Original title:
Life's Meaning, as Told by an Avocado

Copyright © 2025 Creative Arts Management OÜ
All rights reserved.

Author: Sebastian Whitmore
ISBN HARDBACK: 978-1-80566-252-5
ISBN PAPERBACK: 978-1-80566-547-2

Stirring the Soul

I roll around in kitchens bright,
With guacamole, I'm quite the sight.
But oh, the fuss, the toast parade,
By breakfast's end, I'm half-decayed.

They spread me thin, they spread me wide,
In sandwiches, I take great pride.
Yet here I sit, in shadow's thrall,
A dish without a dinner call.

The Natural Balance

Why, I'm green gold, a fruit divine,
With zest as sharp as lemon's line.
But when the salad's lacking cheer,
I'm the hero that they revere.

A sprinkle here, a drizzle there,
I bridge the gap, I'm debonair.
Though often tossed in blender's whirl,
Inside, I shine—just give a twirl!

In Search of the Perfect Pair

They say I need a mate that's sweet,
A salsa spicy, quite the treat.
Yet all I find in closing fray,
Are tortilla chips that fade away.

Oh, where's the zest, the dance, the flair?
Not just a scoop, but love to share!
In crowded bowls, I seek and yearn,
For that perfect crunch, my heart will burn.

A Slice of Harmony

Slice me gently, don't be rash,
I'm far more than just green mash.
On tacos or on pizza crust,
My soft appeal is simply a must.

Let's celebrate this veggie trend,
In every meal, I'm a good friend.
So grab a fork, let's make a scene,
Together we're the avocado cream!

Slices of Serenity

In a bowl so bright and green,
Avocados shine, a feast unseen.
With toast and salt, they dance and cheer,
Making breakfast dreams appear.

Gauguin would paint them, you know well,
In colors that make your taste buds swell.
They're not just spread, but also a vibe,
Finding joy in every tribe.

Between the Pit and the Peel

Life's a pit, they often say,
But guac makes worries fade away.
Between the peel and the creamy bliss,
Is where you find the secret kiss.

A little lime, a dash of spice,
Each bite's a gamble, a roll of dice.
So peel them back, and take a chance,
With every slice, give joy a dance.

Lessons from a Creamy Core

In the center lies a lesson true,
Not just for snacks, but life's debut.
The creamy core doesn't fear decay,
It simply shares its green ballet.

Cut too deep? You'll find a bruise,
But every blemish has its muse.
So roll with it, and don't you fret,
Even the squishy stands for pet.

Laying on bread or rising high,
An avocado can make you fly.
Just spread your wings, and have a bite,
Making the mundane feel so right.

Avocado Epiphanies

While pondering life in a soft embrace,
I learned from an avocado's grace.
Not every pit needs to be ignored,
Sometimes the flaws can be adored.

Slice it smooth, or mash it down,
It brightens up the dullest frown.
With every scoop, a giggle bursts,
In each green spoon, a joy thirsts.

So grab your knife, let's carve away,
Every doubt, every gray dismay.
For in the laughter of guac's good times,
We find the punchline in life's rhymes.

An Unsung Hero

In the fridge, I sit quite still,
Hero of snacks, I save the meal.
With chips I'm the star, that's my game,
But no one knows my humble name.

I'm green and smooth, a creamy delight,
While others get all the culinary hype.
But spread me thin, and watch them cheer,
An avocado steals the show, my dear!

The Guacamole Chronicles

Gathering together, a festive feast,\nChopping tomatoes,
my work increased.
Mash, blend, a squeeze of lime,
Guac on the table, it's guacamole time!

With garlic and salt, I become divine,
As chip after chip, they cross that line.
But when they've scooped out all of me,
They leave a pit — can't they see?

The Art of Ripening

Hanging out on the counter, I await,
For the moment I'll find my perfect state.
A little squeeze, a gentle caress,
I'll be ready to impress, I must confess.

With sunlight and time, I go from green,
To soft and smooth, a glorious scene.
But rush me, please don't make me sad,
An overripe avocado is just plain bad!

Lessons from the Tree

From roots so deep, I learn to grow,
Patience is key, let it show.
Though the world may rush with zest,
Every avocado needs its rest.

So when you're stressed, take a break,
Like me on a branch, for goodness' sake.
Breathe in, breathe out, find your groove,
Just like a fruit, find your smooth move!

The Green Plate Blues

On toast I lie, so smug and bright,
With salt and lime, I feel just right.
A sprinkle here, a smear, a thrill,
I'm popular now, the king of quill.

But wait, I feel a sudden dread,
Too many bites, I'm almost dead!
Pineapple dreams in salsa stew,
Oh, guacamole, what's wrong with you?

Awakening from the Stone

Once a hard shell, I longed to see,
Transformed by warmth, set deeply free.
I rolled to the light, and what a surprise,
I'm creamy and smooth; oh, how time flies!

With chips I dance in the moonlight's gaze,
Twirling in kitchens, a buttery craze.
From neglected to loved, all for the taste,
C'mon, dear folks, let's not go to waste!

Conversations with Guacamole

We sat in the bowl, deep in a chat,
Discussing the merits of lime, and fat.
"Am I your favorite or just your side?"
"Oh, how I relish this joyful ride!"

We laughed 'til we cried, what a fruity scene,
A mash-up of flavors, in hues of green.
"But hold on tight, there's chips up ahead,
Let's make a splatter, let's scatter, let's spread!"

Embracing the Flesh

Peel me gently, with careful hands,
For beneath this skin, a treasure stands.
With every scoop, I bring delight,
Spread on bread, I'm everyone's bite.

In a salad bowl, I twirl and sway,
A jolly green fellow, come join the play!
So if you find a fleshy friend,
Remember, my fun is never to end!

Between Two Halves

In the bowl, I sit so ripe,
A toast to my creamy type.
With a squeeze of lime, I shine,
Oh, what a spread, divine!

Some say I'm a guacamole star,
While others savor me from afar.
I'm more than just a dip, you see,
I'm the life of the party, whee!

The Avocado Encore

I once dreamed of being toast,
Now I'm just the brunch host.
I steal the show, say cheers!
A splash of salt, no fears.

The knife slides through with grace,
I wear my pit like a crown in place.
When I'm sliced, I bring delight,
In the fridge, I must fight the fright!

From Grove to Heart

Born in a grove in the sun,
Dreaming of meals, oh what fun!
Plucked right when I'm just right,
Now I'm ready to take flight.

My journey's a zest-filled thrill,
From tree to plate, I've got the will.
With a smile, I unite the crew,
All embrace the green delight—who knew?

Slices of Perspective

One slice says 'let's eat', it's great,
While another debates on fate.
Am I just a trendy fad?
Or a creamy friend to be had?

With every bite, wisdom unfolds,
Even as my skin turns old.
Laughter's shared with each spread,
Life's just better with avocado bread!

The Dance of the Avocado

On the counter, I sway with glee,
Ripeness spreads joy, just wait and see.
Skin so green, I'm ready to shine,
Join the fiesta, let's have some lime!

All my friends, we're guac-ing up,
Chips and laughter fill every cup.
Dance like nobody's watching, it's true,
Just beware of the knife—ouch! Yikes! Boo-hoo!

Texture of Tranquility

Smooth as silk, oh, feel this bliss,
Spread me on toast, you won't want to miss.
A sprinkle of salt, a dash of zest,
In this calm bite, we are blessed.

Beneath the skin, there's joy to find,
A world of flavors that perfectly bind.
In the bowl, we bask and float,
With every scoop, we'll happily gloat.

A Pit's Perspective

I sit in the middle, round as can be,
Waiting for someone to notice me.
I dream of a plant, where I can thrive,
One little sprout, that's how I strive!

But here in the salad, life isn't so bad,
I'm passed around, though it drives me mad.
A party of greens, I'm the seed of delight,
Just don't mash me up—oh what a fright!

Green Journeys

From tree to table, it's quite a ride,
Fumbling with forks, it's a slippery glide.
Adventures await in every dip,
With spicy salsa, let's take a trip!

Exploring the world on plates and wraps,
Rolling with tacos, oh, what a lapse!
Together we flourish, create and blend,
In every meal, we're the true friends.

Echoes of Vitality

In the garden, green and bright,
Avocados dance, in morning light.
Their smooth skins shine, a joyful scene,
Creating laughter, a guac-filled dream.

With every slice and tasty spread,
They whisper tales of joy instead.
Witty thoughts in every bite,
A funny fruit, oh what a sight!

Nature's Canvas

Nature paints in shades of green,
Avocados reign, a royal scene.
Smashing dreams on toast they flaunt,
A quirky feast, a vibrant jaunt.

With lime's zing, they laugh and prime,
Every bowl a food-based rhyme.
In their world, the funny flows,
An artful meal, as humor grows.

A Flavorful Story

Once an avocado, round and bold,
Dreamed of guacamole, stories told.
With cilantro's help, they found their voice,
In every dip, the world would rejoice.

Through nachos' crunch, they take a stand,
A tangy tale, so grand, so bland.
In kitchens loud, they rule the day,
A flavorful journey, come what may.

The Stillness of Ripeness

In the bowl, they sit in grace,
Plump and perfect, a green embrace.
Waiting for toast, they play so cool,
A stillness that defies all rules.

With a wink of lime, they come alive,
In each bite, the giggles thrive.
Ripeness holds secrets, quite absurd,
A quiet jest, without a word.

The Waiting Game

In the bowl we twirl and spin,
Waiting for the sun to win.
Snoozing in the kitchen mind,
Hoping to be ripe, not blind.

Shiny skin and nature's treasure,
What a life, oh, what a pleasure!
Tick-tock, the days go by,
Will I be breakfast, oh my, oh my?

Everyone passes, glances quick,
Humans hoping for that perfect pick.
So many salads yet to grace,
Just need some love, a little space.

In the end, it's just a game,
Sliced on toast, my shining fame.
I'll strut my stuff, don't need a claim,
This wait was worth it, oh what a name!

Whispers of the Avocado

In silent groves, we hold a chat,
Green dreams brew, just like a spat.
Peel back layers, what do you see?
A world of guac, just let it be!

Little seeds that spark delight,
In every bite, there's pure insight.
"Spread the love," we sing with glee,
Turn your toast into a spree!

Banter with the tomatoes near,
"Who's the best?" they joke and leer.
With every scoop, a tale unfolds,
Of quirky days and friendships bold.

So grab your knife and fork with zest,
In this fruit game, we are the best.
Listen close, you'll hear our call,
A tasty life, come one, come all!

Vines of Connection

From tree to table, we take a ride,
The journey's fun, come join the vibe.
On bread or chips, we find our friends,
Every dip, a story blends.

Twisting roots all intertwined,
A guacamole heart combined.
Laughing as we spread around,
In every bite, sweet joy is found.

"Hey there, salsa," I sing along,
Together we make a zesty song.
Flavor notes and colors brag,
Our friendship won't turn into a drag.

So gather 'round, let's have a feast,
Where joy is served, and laughs increase.
In this vine of love we thrive,
Together as one, we feel alive!

Green and Gold: A Tale

A tale of green in gold attire,
Fashion tips that do inspire!
Soft and creamy, I take a stand,
On brunch tables, where I'm in demand.

Yellow yolks, and bread so warm,
Together we create a charm.
Beneath the sun, I softly glow,
In every bite, the smiles bestow.

"Why so smooth?" the toast does tease,
With every spread, we aim to please.
My golden heart, a treasure bold,
In this world, I've struck gold.

So here's to joy in every meal,
This merry fruit, oh what a steal!
Growing fine, let's raise a cheer,
Green and gold, we persevere!

Roots and Branches

In the garden, I sprout wide,
With roots that dig and confide.
I wiggle and dance to the sun,
Growing dreams, oh what fun!

Branching out to share my ways,
With jokes that brighten dull days.
To be green is a grand affair,
Let's guac it out without a care!

Reflections in a Halved Sphere

Cut me open, see the light,
Half my world is pure delight.
With a pit that's tough, oh so round,
In my flesh, joy's abound.

Friends gather near to taste and share,
With salty chips, we show we care.
In every scoop, laughter spreads,
Each bite's a smile, no room for dread.

To Be Soft and Whole

Firm on the outside, soft within,
A bumpy ride, oh let's begin!
I roll with life, no need to fight,
It's all about the spread tonight.

As toast gets warm and butter flies,
Together we bloom under the skies.
In every mash, a giggle flows,
The cream of the crop is how it goes!

The Unseen Layers of Being

Peel me back, layer by layer,
Discover truths that we can share.
Underneath, there's charm and wit,
In every slice, our spirits lit.

Don't judge me by the skin I wear,
Taste my heart, and you will dare.
For there's a party we invite,
In every bowl, it feels just right!

Ripening Thoughts

In the bowl of time, I start to grow,
Dreaming of sandwiches, just so you know.
Sunshine kisses, I bask in the glow,
A little patience, that's how to flow.

As I mellow, the clock ticks slow,
Salsa on the side, stealing the show.
With each green layer, my wisdom will show,
Being just right, that's how I roll.

The Pit of Existence

In my core, it's hard to define,
The weight of the world is a heavy line.
Sometimes I wonder, am I just divine?
Or just a snack for a hungry feline?

As I ponder these thoughts, I sit back and chill,
Pits are deep, yet I'm tasty still.
Caught in the salad, oh what a thrill,
In this fruit bowl, I'll always fulfill.

Journey of a Hass

From tree to table, it's quite the ride,
Life has its ups and its slippery slide.
Winding through kitchens, I take it in stride,
A guacamole hero, with avocado pride.

Friends with the chips, they dance in delight,
Spreading my goodness, what a sight!
Unpeel my layers, oh what a bite,
In the heart of a dip, everything feels right.

Guacamole Dreams

In my dreams, I'm salsa's king,
Dancing with lime, it's a flavorful fling.
With tomatoes and spices, together we sing,
A fiesta of taste, let the good times swing!

Oh, the bowls we fill, like treasures untold,
Avocados unite, we're worth more than gold.
In every mash-up, new stories unfold,
In the kitchen of laughter, we'll never grow old.

Soulful Slices

In the bowl, I smile wide,
Creamy dreams, you can't hide.
Every bite, a laughter spree,
Life's a feast, come join with me.

Pit in the center, it's my heart,
Not just food, but an art!
Spread my joy on toasts so bright,
Every slice, a pure delight.

Growing Together

In the sun, I stretch and grow,
Learning things I didn't know.
Friends with beans and peas around,
In this patch, happiness found.

Roots in soil, we dig in deep,
Sharing secrets, we don't keep.
A funny crew, we laugh and play,
Growing stronger, day by day.

Green Dreams and Golden Moments

In my dreams, just green and gold,
Stories of flavors yet untold.
Smiling at the sunlit skies,
Dancing in my leafy highs.

Moments wrapped in guacamole,
Fun with chips, it's never lonely!
Each dip brings a cheerful cheer,
Together munching, spreading cheer.

The Heart Beneath the Skin

Peeling back the layers fine,
We reveal the heart, divine.
With every scoop, there's joy to see,
The pit holds laughter, can't you see?

Joining picnics, we share the plate,
Together we celebrate fate.
Cracking jokes under the sun,
In our green world, we have fun!

Nourishment from Within

In the green heart, a treasure stirs,
Rich and buttery, in ripe reassures.
With a dash of salt, and squeeze of lime,
I find my purpose, one slice at a time.

Peel back the layers, feel the embrace,
Of creamy delight, a joyful space.
Though some may scoff, call me a fruit,
I'm a party of flavor, dressed up to boot.

The Smooth Path of Growth

From humble seed, to shining star,
I roll with the punches, travel afar.
The sun kissed my skin, I soaked in the rays,
And now I'm the toast that brightens your days.

I dance on the branches, take joy in the breeze,
Fulfilling my fate with effortless ease.
Grow taller, grow rounder, oh what a show,
Unlocking my magic, watch how I glow!

A Mosaic of Toppings

On toast or a bowl, I'm not alone,
With tomatoes, and cheese, I claim my throne.
A sprinkle of spice, a drizzle of sauce,
In the garden of flavors, I'm the big boss.

While salsa and chips may join the fun,
I blend with their beats, I'm never outdone.
Guac on my side, oh what a sight,
A fiesta of colors; let's party tonight!

Echoes of the Orchard

In the orchard's embrace, where laughter is born,
I sway with my friends, from dusk until morn.
A blender's hum sings a melody sweet,
Encapsulating joy, in every bite we meet.

The crunch of the chips, the crunch of the day,
We mingle together, in a whimsical way.
So raise up your forks, let's join in this cheer,
For in every scoop, there's magic right here.

Beneath the Avocado Moon

Under the avocado moon,
I ponder all my dreams,
With guacamole whispers,
And salsa night-time schemes.

The pit's a heavy burden,
It rolls with every laugh,
But shall I toss it wiser,
Or turn it into guffaws?

Oh, creamy green delight,
A treasure on the vine,
I smile at life's oddities,
And munch on toast divine.

Harmony in a Bowl

In a bowl of fresh delight,
We mingle, twist, and turn,
With tomatoes on the side,
Our friendship's fire will burn.

A sprinkle of the lime zest,
Adds zing to all our talks,
While chips await the dip fest,
Worry not, just relax!

The crunch and creamy dance,
A culinary affair,
In every savory glance,
The taste of joy we share.

The Cycle of Nature

From tree to table, what a ride,
I watched my siblings fall,
In salads and on plates we glide,
Our journey's not so small.

With sunshine ripening our skin,
The world awaits our fate,
But when the bowl's too full of kin,
We laugh, we celebrate!

Oh, every pit has purpose,
And every slice a role,
Together we make perfect sense,
From tree to toss, we're whole.

Seasons of Creaminess

Spring brings a ripened cheer,
While summer adds that zest,
In autumn we spread love here,
And winter? It's the best!

With every scoop a memory,
A burst of joy and cream,
In toast or dip, we dance with glee,
Oh, Life's a tasty dream!

And when my time is done,
And I'm a memory too,
My legacy's the laughter spun,
In every bite of you!

Avocado Affection

In the tree I hang, so plump and green,
Waiting for toast to make me queen.
With a sprinkle of salt, oh what a scene,
I'll charm your taste buds, like a cuisine machine.

Smoother than butter, I'm quite the catch,
Spread me on bread, watch flavors match.
In salads or spreads, I'll never batch,
You'll savor each bite, I'm your snacking patch.

From nachos to sushi, I fit right in,
A party favorite, it's a guaranteed win.
Don't judge my color, or my squishy skin,
For I'm full of good fats, let the feast begin!

So grab a spoon, let's dig right in,
With guacamole love, let's adopt a grin.
In every pop culture meme, I fit like a pin,
This avocado affection, let the good times spin!

A Slice of Time

Time ticks away, but I stay the same,
Ripening slowly, it's all just a game.
In the fridge, I ponder, am I too lame?
But on your plate, I'll bring the fame.

Just wait a bit longer, don't rush my fate,
Too hard to eat? Oh, what a debate!
But catch me just right, it's a perfect state,
A slice of pure joy when it's on your plate.

Peel back my skin, what do you see?
A creamy delight, as smooth as can be.
From salads to spreads, I'm basically free-be,
Embracing each moment, living carefree.

So slice me up, and pass me around,
I'm the life of the party, I make no sound.
In the symphony of meals, I'm the joyful pound,
A slice of good vibes in your kitchen found!

The Journey from Grove to Table

From grove to your table, what a wild ride,
Hanging with friends on a leafy slide.
I dream of the moment, I won't need to hide,
Just waiting for you to take me with pride.

It's a game of patience, this avocado life,
From blossom to fruit, it's filled with strife.
But once on your plate, I stir up the hype,
On crackers or tacos, I'm your flavor type.

I cross oceans and trucks, feeling like a star,
Just to brighten your breakfast or fancy Bazaar.
I'm the cool green touch and I'm never bizarre,
An avocado's journey, it's a culinary afar.

So cherish this trip from the seed to the spread,
Each bite's a reminder to not rush ahead.
With laughter and joy, let's keep the fun fed,
From grove to table, let's celebrate bread!

Growing in Quietude

In the orchard where I silently shine,
The sun warms my skin, oh how divine!
I'm a gentle giant, growing in line,
With hopes of delighting, a taste so fine.

While others may rush, I take my sweet time,
Swaying with breezes, in rhythm and rhyme.
In the peace of the grove, I slowly climb,
Filling up with love, I'm a fruity prime.

You may think I'm calm, but inside I jest,
Waiting for ripeness, I'm on a quest.
With every passing moment, I do my best,
To be the green treasure in your tasty zest.

So here's to the quiet, the still and the slow,
In patience and calm, the best fruits will grow.
Laughing with joy as we savor the show,
Growing in quietude, letting good vibes flow!

The Green Heart's Whisper

In a world of toast and cheese,
An avocado aims to please.
With a pit that's firm yet round,
It whispers secrets, profound.

Don't judge by skin, it's what's within,
A creamy heart, where tales begin.
With humor rich and zest so bold,
These funny fruits have stories told.

Slice me open, watch me shine,
In salads, I do just fine.
With each dip, a laugh you'll find,
Smash my dreams, but I won't mind.

So next time you're feeling blue,
Remember green, and laugh anew.
For in this bowl, so ripe and sweet,
Laughter's spread—let joy repeat.

Guacamole Dreams

In a bowl where flavors dance,
An avocado takes a chance.
With lime and salt, it jumps right in,
Creating dreams, let fun begin!

A mash of green, a party vibe,
Add some onion, then we jibe.
With chips in hand, we're all a team,
In this dip, we chase the dream.

But wait, oh no! The pit's in sight,
You took a turn, it's not quite right.
A slippery tale of guac's delight,
Makes every bite—an epic fight!

So pass the bowl, let's make a cheer,
For every smash, we hold so dear.
In this kitchen, where dreams combine,
Laughter and guac are truly divine.

Beneath the Skin: A Journey of Seeds

Beneath my skin, a tale unwinds,
Of sunny days and gentle winds.
With each bite, a story flows,
Of how it grew, as laughter grows.

A pit so grand, a tale to share,
In wraps and tacos, it finds its flair.
Through salads bright and salsas known,
This little green has truly grown.

From market stalls to kitchen scenes,
I dream of toast and silly memes.
With every scoop, a giggle blooms,
As flavors swirl in vibrant rooms.

So join me here, let's have some fun,
In every bite, we've just begun.
A journey deep, through laughs and seeds,
In every meal, fulfillment leads.

A Stone's Silent Wisdom

In the center lies a stone,
The wisdom that can stand alone.
It knows the jokes, the puns, the glee,
Of guacamole and jubilee.

Though green and soft, it's got some sass,
A party fruit that's full of class.
With laughter spry like lemon zest,
It hides a truth you can digest.

When mashed and spread, it finds its way,
To all our hearts, come what may.
With every meal, a giggly toast,
To avocados we love the most!

So here's to you, my funny friend,
In every dish, our hearts you mend.
Together we'll laugh, and that's the key,
In the land of green, we all agree!

The Smoothness of Being

In a world so ripe and round,
I glide through life, no worry found.
With a pit that's snug and tight,
I relish each delicious bite.

Embrace the toast, spread it wide,
With each smear, I take great pride.
Crispy edges, creamy core,
A sprinkle of salt, and I want more!

I dodge the knife with crafty flair,
A sliced-up joke to share and spare.
With every scoop and every laugh,
I find my joy, my perfect path.

Though I might get brown with time,
In guacamole, I still shine.
A funky fruit, with charm on deck,
In this big bowl, I'm the true spec!

Subtle Flavors of Existence

Peel me back, take a peek,
Beneath the surface lies the cheek.
Life's a party on your plate,
These flavors blend, and that's our fate.

In a salad, I get tossed,
In a dip, I'm never lost.
Every bite, a little dance,
With every crunch, there's a chance!

I'm not just green, oh what a sin,
I bring folks together and always win.
From tacos tight to sushi rolls,
I'm the secret to happy souls.

So when you munch, think of me,
The fruit of joy, so carefree.
In this crazy, zesty ride,
I'll be your guide, right by your side!

A Green Embrace

In my skin, there's warmth and cheer,
Feeling good from ear to ear.
Soft and squishy, oh so sweet,
Embraced by toast, life's a treat!

Hold me tight, let's blend away,
With every mash, we laugh and play.
In a bowl, I find my crowd,
Mix it up, oh it's allowed!

Sometimes I wear a little brown,
But in salsa, I'll never frown.
Dipped in chips, such a delight,
Together, we'll dance through the night!

Forever fruity, always fun,
Grab a fork, let's eat, let's run!
In the moments that we share,
Open your heart, let's be a pair!

The Harmony of Guacamole

Whisk me up in a joyful whirl,
A splash of lime, a twist, a twirl.
With every scoop, laughter flows,
In this bowl, we find our prose.

Tomato bits, a dash of spice,
Stir it gently, oh so nice.
We blend our dreams and hopes so bright,
In this guac, we take our flight!

Friends gather round, ready to feast,
In these moments, we're all released.
Add a chip, and let it dip,
In this quirky, tasty trip!

As the night goes and laughter grows,
With our guacamole, joy just flows.
Here's to fun, a life fulfilled,
In every bite, our hearts are thrilled!

The Kaleidoscope of Taste

In the bowl, you twirl so bright,
Colors dance, a tasty sight.
Guacamole dreams, oh what a ride,
Mash and spread, let joy abide.

With lime and salt, you steal the show,
A party starter, steal the flow.
Friends gather 'round for a dip or two,
In this fiesta, there's joy anew.

Slice you thick, arrayed with care,
On tacos and salads, you love to share.
A slice of heaven on my plate,
In every meal, you're simply great!

Oh avocado, you're such a tease,
With a buttery kiss, you're sure to please.
Every bite, a hearty cheer,
You're the star of snacks, green and dear!

Within the Avocado's Embrace

Soft and green, a silky treat,
Hugging toast, oh, what a feat!
Smash it gently, don't make a mess,
In every bite, pure happiness!

Wrapped in skins, you snuggle tight,
A treasure found in morning light.
Breakfast joy, you make me grin,
With every slice, let the fun begin!

Chillin' on the counter, waiting so long,
Colorful fruits sing you a song.
Patience tested, oh what a game,
For your embrace, I stake my claim!

You're the reason I love to brunch,
On bagels and wraps, you pack a punch.
Oh, green delight, you're heavenly bold,
In every moment, your warmth I hold!

The Pathway to Flavor

You glide on chips like a dreamy wave,
Bringing joy, oh how you behave!
In sandwiches, you spread the cheer,
A creamy life, it's crystal clear!

Rolling with salsas, a zesty buddy,
Your charm shines bright, never muddy.
Every dip and swirl sings delight,
You make every party just feel right!

Smashed or sliced, you can't go wrong,
Every meal, you're where I belong.
A sprinkle of spice, a twist of lime,
With every bite, you're simply sublime!

You're the reason avocados thrive,
Filling hearts, keeping taste alive.
Dance on my plate, a vibrant show,
Dear friend, I love you more than you know!

Beyond the Toast

Beyond bread, you boldly stride,
In salads, burritos, you take pride.
Dancing with flavors, not shy at all,
In every dish, you have a ball!

With smooth accents, you bring the flair,
A culinary hug, beyond compare.
Blending with fruits, you're quite the blend,
Every meal, you're a trusty friend!

Even sushi rolls adore your face,
Wrapped in seaweed, you hold your place.
A twist of zest, a sprinkle free,
In every bite, you're pure glee!

Oh avocado, you've conquered the scene,
With laughter and tastes, forever keen.
From tacos to bowls, you claim the prize,
In the great taste game, you're always a surprise!

A Journey in Cream

In the orchard, I hang tight,
Bright green dreams in morning light.
With a pit, I carry weight,
Growing hopes, they won't abate.

Toast me once or maybe thrice,
Spread me gently, oh so nice.
In every bite, a smile blooms,
Who knew fruit could chase the glooms?

Life's a pit, and I'm the scoop,
In guacamole, we all loop.
Laugh with friends in salad bowls,
Mashing worries, feeding souls.

From tree to table, it's a race,
Sliced or blended, find your place.
Let's enjoy this creamy ride,
With each bite, we feel the pride.

Musings in the Pulp

Peeking out from leafy green,
Pondering what might have been.
I'm not just a pretty treat,
In my flesh, life's secrets meet.

Who knew dinner could be fun?
A drizzle of oil and we're done.
From mundane to gourmet flair,
I'm the star, a fruit so rare.

Remember strangers at the bar?
Creating chaos with my jar.
Two avocados, tales unfold,
About the joys of being bold.

In salads, I find my bliss,
A little lime, oh what a kiss.
Laughing in a zesty dance,
In every bite, there's pure romance.

Subtle Flavors of Being

Beneath the skin, my secrets dwell,
In every scoop, a hidden spell.
Some think I'm just for the toast,
But in soups, I'm quite the host.

I joke with lemons near the squeeze,
Unlocking joy, an art to please.
Slice me thin, or blend me loud,
In every dish, I'm feeling proud.

Life's complex, I must confess,
But with a sprinkle, I feel blessed.
In wraps or dips, I take a stand,
Whirling thoughts, a creamy band.

I dance in bowls, with chips align,
Spreading laughter, a love divine.
With friends and chip, let's take a taste,
In every bite, let's not waste!

Nurtured by Soil

Roots so deep in earth so fine,
Sipping sunshine, feeling divine.
From humble seed to grand delight,
I'm here to make your day more bright.

With soil hugs, I start to grow,
Funny twists in all my dough.
Add a pinch of salt, a laugh,
Mixing joy with every half.

In the kitchen, I play chef,
Wit and flavor, a clever riff.
Bring the heat, just let me mash,
With every dream, a silly splash.

So here's to all who take a bite,
Join my ride, from morn 'til night.
Together we'll create a spread,
Sharing smiles and daily bread.

A Symphony in Green

In a garden where I grow,
Softly in the sun's warm glow.
Friends and foes, a pit's embrace,
Together in this leafy space.

Salsa dreams and guacamole nights,
Swinging free with all delights.
Melody of zest and cheer,
Who knew avocados could be dear?

Ripen slow, I take my time,
Each moment feels like a rhyme.
Facing dips and tasty spreads,
A symphony, where joy simply spreads.

So raise a toast, let laughter swell,
In every bite, a tale to tell.
Though homes may call us guac and dip,
We sing of love with every sip.

Moods of an Avocado

Today I'm smooth, just feeling fine,
Tomorrow, might be guAC your mind.
Sometimes I'm green, sometimes I'm brown,
In every mood, I wear my crown.

Chilling in a bowl, a bright display,
Tomorrow I'll be spread for play.
All my friends in tacos join,
A feast where joy is never coin.

When I feel ripe, I'm all the rage,
But watch me age, I'm like a sage.
Limon and salt, the zest to share,
In every slice, I'm full of flair.

So grab a chip, or bake with me,
In every dish, I long to be.
An avocado cheer, a fun guise,
Life has zest in every slice!

A Toast to the Unseen

In the bowl, I sit with glee,
My green skin's a mystery.
Sliced and spread on toast so fine,
Here's to love, and good design!

Oh, how I envy the big pits,
They steal the show with their sitting bits.
While I blend into dips with pride,
Let's raise a toast, let's enjoy the ride!

With each scoop and every bite,
You know I'm the star of the night.
My soft charm holds friendships tight,
In guacamole, we unite!

So here's to us, the avos bold,
In salads, spreads, a joy to hold.
A tiny fruit with dreams so grand,
Making happy times, hand in hand.

The Taste of Togetherness

Mashed or sliced, I'm here to stay,
Bringing smiles in my own way.
With chips and friends, I take my chance,
To show the world how we can dance!

A dash of lime, a pinch of salt,
A food party, I'm the vault.
When folks gather, I take my seat,
The center stage, it tastes so sweet!

Oh, what fun, in tacos, too,
How can one stop at just a few?
The taste of love in every bite,
Together, we shine, oh what a sight!

Safety in numbers, that's my goal,
In every bowl, I find my role.
So spread the joy with zest and cheer,
Together we thrive, let's raise a beer!

Cresting Waves of Green

Waves of green, I'm here to roll,
A creamy wave that soothes the soul.
On smoothies and toast, I make my mark,
A fruity gem in a world so stark!

From the tree to the table, I take a dive,
Making each dish come alive.
Blessed by the sun and kissed by rain,
I ask for nothing, it's all in the game!

In salads, I float like a buoy,
A taste that whispers, 'hey, enjoy!'
Each little scoop, a joyous ride,
Surfing through flavors, side by side.

Let's spread the joy, let's make some noise,
In every home, I'm one of the joys.
With a squeeze of lime and friends all around,
In waves of green, our laughs abound.

Reflections from the Orchard

In the orchard, I dream and sway,
Gazing at clouds, I'm here to play.
Hanging high, I soak up the sun,
Reflecting joy, oh what fun!

Shining bright in the morning light,
I whisper secrets, oh so slight.
When the harvest comes, we celebrate,
As laughter grows, it feels just great!

A hint of salt or a sprinkle sweet,
My presence makes the day complete.
With every bite, stories unfold,
In the orchard, let's be bold!

So grab a fork, come share a dream,
Let's savor life, a joyful theme.
Together we'll feast, come one, come all,
In the orchard of laughter, we always stand tall!

Beneath the Bump: Nature's Insights.

In a world that spins so fast,
I ponder questions, unsurpassed.
With a pit so round, I take a seat,
And wonder how I'm so unique.

Branches sway and birds will sing,
While I just sit, awaiting spring.
With every squeeze, I feel the jam,
Is this my fate? Am I a spam?

Life's a toast, and I'm the spread,
On crunchy bread, I'm well-fed.
While folks debate what's ripe or not,
I just chill in my cozy spot.

So guacamole, or just plain?
I take it easy, free from strain.
With laughter, I'll roll through the day,
As a humble fruit, I'll find my way.

The Essence of Green

Oh, to be vibrant and so bright,
I shine like emeralds in the light.
While people search for deeper clues,
I blend in salads, what a ruse!

With a twist here and a slice there,
I'm the star, beyond compare.
I dodge the bad jokes, play it cool,
With my green skin, nothing's cruel.

While humans ponder, scheme, and plot,
I roll with the punches—give it a shot.
Just a fruit, but much to give,
In dips and spreads, oh, how I live!

So here's to the essence, pure and grand,
For in each bite, a tale so planned.
With zest and fun, I'll never tire,
I'm just a fruit, igniting desire!

Beneath the Skin

Underneath this rugged shell,
Lies a treasure, can't you tell?
Creamy goodness, smooth and bright,
I bring smiles, day and night.

While folks debate with endless zeal,
What to dress me with—oh, the appeal!
With every scoop, they take a chance,
To dance with flavors, oh what a dance!

Am I a topping or the main?
With all this love, I've much to gain.
Between tomatoes and some lime,
I just add joy, every time!

So spread me 'round, on toast or chip,
In every bite, let laughter trip.
For beneath the skin, you see the tune,
A melody of joy that makes hearts swoon!

A Seed's Whisper

In the heart of me, a secret lies,
A tiny seed, where hope complies.
Whispers of growth, laughter near,
I tell the tales only fruits hear.

With sun and rain, I take my flight,
To green the world—what a delight!
As folks debate, oh what to do,
I just laugh, it's all so true!

I'll sprout opinions, crude yet fun,
In every dish, I am the pun.
While kitchens buzz with zest and flair,
I simply smile, a gift to share.

So here's to seeds, and growth so weird,
In every laugh, a truth is steered.
Join in the fun, taste and define,
For I'm the fruit that's simply divine!

The Dance of Ripeness

In a grove where sunlight beams,
Avocados plot their creamy dreams.
They wiggle, jiggle, ready to sway,
Just waiting for the perfect day.

They gather round, it's quite a sight,
Discussing guacamole with delight.
Each day brings a new delight,
To be smooth and ripe, oh what a plight!

Some play it cool, still a bit green,
While others boast of being unseen.
They know that soon they'll hit the plate,
And oh, what joy to meet their fate!

So here's to the ripest of them all,
Their dance a quirky avocado ball.
In every bite, a cheer, a grin,
For life's a feast, let's dig right in!

Beyond the Toast: A Philosophical Spread

On morning bread, a spread divine,
Avocado wisdom here to shine.
Creamy thoughts on crispy toast,
Crunchy edges we love the most.

What lies within this green delight?
Is it magic, or just good bites?
Philosophers gather with forks in hand,
To ponder what's truly grand.

They muse on flavor, texture, and hue,
And giggle at the thoughts they brew.
With every spread, a laugh to share,
Avocados teach us how to care.

So smear it wide, on every meal,
Laughing with friends, how good it feels!
Beyond the toast, let joy transcend,
In every scoop, find a friend.

An Ode to Velvety Dreams

Oh, avocado, lush and bright,
You bring joy from morning to night.
In bowls and salads, you reign supreme,
A velvety dream, the ultimate theme.

Slice you gently, like a work of art,
You touch our bellies, you touch our heart.
With each soft scoop, laughter's embraced,
In your creamy depths, we find our place.

From sushi rolls to smoothies so bold,
Your tales of taste are yet untold.
In every meal, a dash of cheer,
We eat and giggle, year after year.

So here's to you, the lovely green,
In every kitchen, you reign as queen.
An ode to you, with every bite,
Life's brightest delight, our purest light!

Avocado Alchemy

In a world of mash, a secret art,
Avocado magic plays its part.
With a sprinkle of salt, some lime's embrace,
Transform your meal, enhance its grace.

Guacamole dreams and dip delight,
Turning ordinary into pure delight.
Each spoonful's a potion, a savory spell,
In the pantry's corner, we bid farewell.

Creating wonders, wrapped in green,
A sprinkle of love makes the best cuisine.
With every taste, we find a cheer,
In avocado alchemy, we persevere.

So grab that bowl, let's mix and stir,
A toast to the magic, of this we are sure!
With laughter and joy, we all agree,
Avocados bring us, together with glee!

Reflections in Green

In a bowl I sit, so bright,
Wrapped in green, a funny sight.
Craving toast, or salad's charm,
Yet wait for ripeness, no harm.

Peel me gently, oh so slow,
Inside my flesh, a golden glow.
With every slice, your smile spreads,
Whispers of wisdom in your breads.

Each pit holds secrets, quite obscure,
Yet blended down, I feel demure.
For in guacamole's embrace,
We find our joy, our happy place.

So take a dip, enjoy the spree,
In my essence, let laughs be free.
Who knew a fruit could speak so loud?
Join the party, be avocado proud!

The Bountiful Paradox

I am both creamy and quite tough,
A paradox that's oh so rough.
In every bite, a playful tease,
You'll find me popping out with ease.

Some call me green, some call me gold,
With every scoop, my stories unfold.
A fruit that lives in constant debate,
Are you a side? Or are you great?

From salads to toasts, I play it cool,
In every kitchen, I break the rule.
Though folks may argue, I've made my mark,
Just slice me once, ignite the spark.

So spread me wide, or mash me small,
In this wacky world, I've got it all.
With every dish, may laughter sprout,
For I am fruit that brings folks out!

Taste of the Unseen

Hidden within, the bold delight,
The taste of dreams, both day and night.
Some say I'm smooth, some say I'm hip,
But with a squeeze, I'll make you flip.

In tacos or on nachos high,
I bring the party, oh my my!
With every bite, a little cheer,
A fruit that dances, bright and clear.

Let's not forget, my doppelgänger,
The not-so-ripe, the awkward stanger.
Sometimes I'm hard, and sometimes I'm soft,
But together we laugh, our spirits aloft.

So take a taste, embrace the fun,
In guacamole, we'll never run.
We're just a fruit, but what a spree,
With humor and joy, we set you free!

The Color of Contentment

In kitchens bright, I hold my ground,
With zest and glee, I'm always found.
Green and friendly, I wave hello,
To every dish, I steal the show.

Sliced or smashed, I grace your plate,
A quirky fruit, it's never too late.
You might add lime or a pinch of salt,
But here's my secret – I'm the true vault.

Just roll with me, don't take a stare,
In my embrace, there's joy to spare.
Each hearty scoop, each silly grin,
A taste sensation, let's begin!

So join the dance, and take a chance,
In every bite, let giggles prance.
I'm here to cheer, in every bite,
For avocado's the true delight!

In the Shade of a Tree

In a green cocoon, I dangle high,
Watching the world, I can't deny.
With a pit so round, I'm quite a catch,
Life's quite a ride, with every match.

I've seen some folks, in quite a mess,
Trying to slice me, oh, what a guess!
They think I'm just guacamole bliss,
But I hold secrets, with every kiss.

So let them ponder, so let them pry,
I lounge in comfort, just asking why.
With skin so brilliant, I wear my best,
In every toast, I'm truly blessed.

One day I'm smashed, next on a chip,
Wrapping up tacos, let's take a trip!
What's life without a sprinkle of zest?
Join this green fruit, forget the rest!

Nature's Soft Embrace

Nestled in soil, under the sun,
Feeling each wiggle, it's all just fun.
With leaves in the chorus, I sway and sway,
Nature's tickle calls me out to play.

Don't be alarmed, I've got it charmed,
In this vibrant world, I feel quite armed.
Each plump adventure, I take with glee,
Trust in the process, just let it be!

With every drizzle, my colors ignite,
Dancing with shadows, oh what delight!
Who knew green could be such a show?
In the grand scheme, I'm the star of the show.

When winter chill bites, I won't feel bad,
For soon I'll bounce back, making life glad.
Huddled with friends, we share a good jest,
Together we shine, we're simply the best!

The Wisdom of Ripeness

Oh, to be ripe, it's truly divine,
Waiting for sunshine, a little red wine.
With a pit of wisdom, I know and see,
Each moment counts, just like a spree.

Peel me back slowly, let flavors explode,
What tales I hold, as I lighten your load.
From salad to sandwich, I smooth each bite,
How can you question my sheer delight?

I laugh with the lime, unite with the spice,
Mixing with onions? Now that's precise!
In every dish, I add a grand twist,
To think I was once just a green mist!

So toast to the journey, the joy and the blend,
Like me, be daring, and just transcend.
Life is a banquet, don't hide in the shade,
Embrace the adventure, let laughter cascade!

Layers of Purpose

Peeling my layers, a curious quest,
Searching for meaning, in every zest.
With each tasty slice, I gather my fame,
For all of the dishes that share my name.

On toast or in smoothies, I rule the day,
So many delights, in my own quirky way.
In the lunchbox or brunch, I'm always there,
A goofy green hero, with nary a care.

When folks take a fork, I playfully smile,
Cooking up joy, I stay in style.
Each savory bite, a puzzle to solve,
In the realm of the kitchen, it's me who evolves!

From farm to table, my purpose is clear,
Adding a twist that we all hold dear.
Life's grand adventure, I'll sweeten the path,
With layers of joy, let's burst into laughter!

Ripen in Reflection

In a bowl I sit and think,
With peers who love to wink.
A fuzzy skin, a sturdy core,
What do we exist for more?

Green and smooth, I feel so fine,
Yet ponder how I turn to dine.
Does ripeness come from joy or fright?
Or just how close I am to light?

The Avocado's Paradox

Some say I'm bland, just simply green,
But oh, the flavors I can glean!
From toast to dips, I spread delight,
Yet many choose to flee from sight.

Am I a fruit or simply food?
A paradox that can't be rude.
So when you slice, please take a breath,
And savor all before my death.

A Toast to Existence

On every brunch, I make my mark,
A spread of goodness, quite the spark.
With lime and salt, I come alive,
In every bite, I seem to thrive.

Raise your forks and hold me high,
A toast to all who ask me why.
With every scoop, I like to jest,
For humor is the very best!

The Fruit that Holds Secrets

Within my skin, some secrets dwell,
Muffled whispers, tales to tell.
Am I too smooth, or just a tease?
Peel away and find your keys.

I might be green, but with a twist,
There's deeper thoughts you'd hate to miss.
So crack me open, have a look,
Who knew a fruit could be a book?

www.ingramcontent.com/pod-product-compliance
Lightning Source LLC
Chambersburg PA
CBHW072148200426
43209CB00051B/852